Perfect Presentations

Andrew Leigh and Michael Maynard run Maynard Leigh
Associates, a human resources and development consultancy,
whose mission is unlocking peoples' potential.

Other titles in the *Perfect* series

Perfect
Presentations

Andrew Leigh and Michael Maynard

BOOKS

Published by Random House Books 2009

2 4 6 8 10 9 7 5 3 1

First published in Great Britain in 1993 by Century Business

This edition first published in 2009 by
Random House Books
Random House, 20 Vauxhall Bridge Road,
London SW1V 2SA

www.rbooks.co.uk

Addresses for companies within The Random House Group Limited can be found at: www.randomhouse.co.uk/offices.htm

The Random House Group Limited Reg. No. 954009

A CIP catalogue record for this book
is available from the British Library

ISBN 9781847945518

The Random House Group Limited supports The Forest Stewardship Council
(FSC), the leading international forest certification organisation. All our titles that
are printed on [Greenpeace approved] paper carry the FSC logo.
Our paper procurement policy can be found at
www.rbooks.co.uk

FSC   Mixed Sources
Product group from well-managed
forests and other controlled sources
www.fsc.org   © 1996

Typeset by SX Composing DTP, Rayleigh, Essex
Printed and bound in Great Britain by Bookmarque Ltd, Croydon, CR0 4TD

Milton Keynes Council	
2394669	
Askews	May-2009
658.452 LEI	£6.99

Contents

For
Aiden, Darion and Jonathan

Before you start . . .

What would it be like to deliver a perfect presentation? It would probably exceed your most optimistic plans and expectations. You'd experience one of those wonderful moments where everything seems to go right and you perform at your absolute best. Your audience reacts enthusiastically and comes away inspired.

That's asking a lot and you can't expect it every time. However, it's certainly possible to maximize the chances of it happening, and this book will help.

On offer here are guidance, ideas and plenty of tips and techniques. Only you can decide whether a particular section or exercise is relevant. Skip material that seems inappropriate. Extract value from what looks helpful.

The first section helps you assess your current presenting ability and your commitment to improve. Next come some basic principles about presentations. The following sections explore the essential ingredients of perfect presentations. The first of these, on preparation, is much the longest because more presentations fail through lack of it, than for any other reason.

Much of the material for *Perfect Presentations* stems from our own regular public and company in-house courses. Many major organizations have used these over the years and now you also can gain some of the benefits – at a fraction of the cost!

We want you to enjoy *Perfect Presentations*; it was written with you in mind. We hope it encourages you to give more presentations that are exciting, powerful and creative.

Good luck!

CHAPTER 1

Why we need presentation skills

First, second and third impressions count. How you present yourself matters in so many ways.

Asking for a rise
Being persuasive
Briefing a group
Conducting training
Customer care
Explaining a report
Giving a talk
Making a speech
Obtaining a job
Interviews

Leading a team
Problem solving
Making a decision in a
    group
Running a meeting
Selling a product or
    service
Getting action
Using the phone
Pitching for business

The awful truth
Presentations play an important part in almost every area of work. It's how other people often judge our effectiveness. Presenting well is just as vital outside work too, whether you are addressing a school parents' meeting or giving an after-dinner speech.

More than heights, snakes, disease, financial problems or even death, what many of us fear most is speaking to a group of people. Is that how you feel too? In which case this guide could be the best investment you've made in yourself for a long time.

Your dynamism

Tap into your ability to present well and you also contact your personal power. It's a way of becoming more effective as a human being. Present well and the ramifications are endless. It can unlock other valuable parts of your potential.

Are you wondering 'can I **really** be a dynamic presenter?' Perhaps making an impact seems too difficult? Or do you feel that establishing a personal presence is a mysterious trick belonging only to charismatic people?

If you say 'I can't present well' it becomes true. It sends exactly that message to:

Your subconscious   **Your audience**

It is not inevitable that you give a poor presentation. You've already begun countering this negative message by reading this guide. Or perhaps you already present well and are wondering 'could I really do much better?' Yes! There's *always* a new level of impact to achieve, though it means taking more risks. Yet when it works, WOW!

Did someone at work suggest you could benefit from improving your presentation impact? If so, ask them to discuss **why** they feel it's necessary. For example, if your boss has said you should improve, ask for more specific information. You may learn that unless you do improve your presentation skills, new opportunities, promotion or valuable further experience will be closed to you.

Have you a presentation to give soon? Wouldn't it be wonderful if your audience stood and cheered, or said how well you'd done? Spend a few moments right now, day-dreaming about what fun it would be, to excel at presenting.

The only way to discover the limits of the possible is to go beyond them to the impossible.
Arthur C Clark

You can do it! In the hundreds of workshops we've run, we've never met anyone who cannot significantly improve their presenting impact. It just takes some help and a strong commitment. So you need to know *why* you should improve and some of the problems that can make it seem a waste of time. Spend a few moments filling out the following list.

IMPROVING MY PRESENTATION IMPACT

REASONS FOR	REASONS AGAINST
_____	_____
_____	_____
_____	_____
_____	_____
_____	_____
_____	_____
_____	_____

Do the pros outweigh the cons?
IF NOT, PLEASE HAND THIS GUIDE TO SOME-ONE ELSE WHOM YOU THINK MIGHT BENEFIT MORE FROM IT.

To present better you must:

- Believe it's possible
- Know it's desirable
- Want to make it happen
- Work at it

Treats

The world snooker champion, Steve Davis, prepared for stardom by promising himself a Mars Bar if he potted a certain number of balls from difficult positions on the table. Or he refused a cup of tea until he had practised for a certain amount of time.

Increase your own commitment by promising yourself various rewards for becoming a better presenter. Incentives work when you choose them yourself! For instance, if you complete the rest of this workbook, or actively seek feedback from your next three presentation situations, decide to reward yourself with a definite treat.

It could be anything from a night at the movies to a new stereo, from a meal in your favourite restaurant to a new hat or suit. Choose something that would really get you moving – something you value.

Insight

There are two main ways of becoming a better presenter and you may need both.

- Formal methods – training and guides like this
- Giving presentations

Formal training and reading guides like this give you new information and show possible areas for improvement. In development workshops you have the opportunity to practise and receive feedback on your performance.

The second and more important way is by actually doing live presentations. The more you do, the more you learn. Each time provides an opportunity of obtaining more feedback.

For example, if you want to present yourself more effectively at job interviews it's sometimes quite possible to obtain feedback on your performance by asking for information on how you came across. Similarly, if you speak at a meeting you can explore which part of your performance went well and which could do with improvement, by being willing to ask people for this kind of feedback.

The Impact Log
Try keeping the IMPACT LOG at the end of this guide. Record there information about each presenting experience and rate yourself on various criteria. It provides important cumulative feedback.

Or keep a copy of the Impact Log in your personal organizer and regularly add to it. It takes self-discipline to keep the log going, but when you realize how useful it is for your next presentation, you'll wonder how you did without it.

I do not object to people looking at their watches when I am speaking but I strongly object when they start shaking them to make certain they are still going.
Lord Birkett

Top ups
You may make a spectacular improvement in presenting immediately after reading this guide, watching a training video or attending a formal course. Yet such changes can quickly fade away:

• Regularly re-read parts of this guide

- IF YOU HAVE A VIDEO ON PRESENTATIONS KEEP DIPPING INTO IT
- Attend top-up training courses once or twice a year, constantly to push you to reach and maintain your next level of impact
- Ask other people for feedback regularly

KNOW-HOW

If there are any secrets to presenting well, you'll find them in this guide.

However, you don't become good at tennis or using a computer just by reading about it. Plenty of practical experience is essential.

One way of gaining practical experience in relative privacy is in a skills workshop. The best ones give you a real buzz; during them you are helped to see your potential and find your own unique way to improving your impact. The focus, as in our own **Performing With Presence** workshops, is always on empowerment, not on rules of how to stand, or ways to use a flip chart.

If you're serious about becoming a better presenter, spare some time to attend a workshop.

SUPPORT

In your quest to become a Perfect Presenter, find a way of giving yourself regular support. Can you talk to a friend regularly about your efforts? Can you meet with a group of colleagues who are also trying to improve?

Support pushes you to new levels of performance. It encourages you, questions how you are doing and inspires you to take bigger risks.

PRESENTATION SKILLS CHECK LIST

- Seek regular feedback on your presenting
- To present better you have to
    Believe it's possible
    Know it's desirable
    Want to make it happen
- Work at it. Keep developing your presentations through incentives of your choice.
- Improve through formal training and reading; and actually presenting
- Constantly try to discover what works and what doesn't
- Use the Impact Log at the end of the book to monitor your performance
- Ask people for regular feedback about your presenting
- Obtain constant support

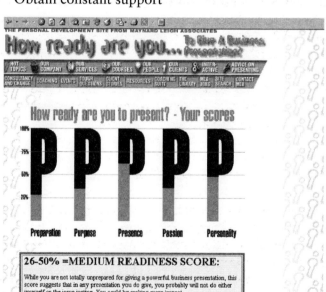

How ready are you to give a business presentation? Test yourself right now by using the internet and going to: http://www.maynardleigh.co.uk/ready.shtml

This easy to use test shows areas where you are weak and ones where you appear strong.

Here for example is the sort of feedback that you will receive. The approach uses the 5 Ps of Presentation that we introduce in Chapter Three.

CHAPTER 2

Basic Principles

Being a powerful presenter is about being yourself, developing your personal style.

How your boss or your favourite speaker performs is not necessarily how you should do it. Every powerful presenter discovers their own way of making an impact.

The best presenters often break all the rules. They may talk or act outrageously and somehow get away with it. Success comes from being themselves, not doing imitations.

Despite their successes, good presenters keep asking:

- What is it that I'm **not** doing?
- What else might work better?

Perfect Presentation rests on these four basic principles:

- Everyone has something to say – including you
- You have ways of communicating belonging just to you
- You have a **right** to be heard
- You are responsible for being heard

Everyone has something to say

Inside everyone there's supposed to be at least one book waiting to be written. You *do* have something special to say – finding it is what becoming a Perfect Presenter is partly about.

Even when you are required to present a pre-arranged company message, a model sales pitch, or a standard talk, inside are your own views, attitudes, beliefs and experiences which can give a special emphasis or slant to what you say.

- The most boring person becomes fascinating when given a chance to talk about what really matters to him or her. There are no really boring people, only boring ways of behaving.

You are unlike any other reader of this guide. Or any other person in this country, indeed the whole world. With your experience, life, beliefs, values, you **always** have something to offer. You are unique.

No two people speak exactly alike, even identical twins differ. Just for fun, try imagining:

'Yes, we have no bananas!' being said by . . .

Your boss	Archbishop of Canterbury
Sylvester Stallone	The Queen
Supermarket checker	Familiar TV character
The Prime Minister	Waiter in a Greek restaurant
Your best friend	The plumber

Now *you* say it aloud a couple of times – you're not the same as them – you're unique.

Electronic voice prints prove each person's voice is special. No two voices are identical. Nuances, inflections, emphasis, timing, volume, pitch make each of us special.

Nor is voice your only unique asset. Body, eyes, head, hands, feet all create your personal communication style. What you say, when you say it and to whom, add further differences.

You have a right to be heard

Many of our life experiences may have implanted a belief that we have no right to be heard. Test your present attitude to being heard:

Invent five reasons why each of the following people should listen to you, at least briefly:

The President of
Ford Motors   _____

_____   _____

_____   _____

Your bank manager   _____

_____   _____

_____   _____

The most senior person
in your organization   _____

_____   _____

_____   _____

The audience at your
next presentation   _____

_____   _____

_____   _____

Someone you admire   _____

_____   _____

_____   _____

If it's hard to find five good reasons keep working at it!
Remember, **YOU HAVE A RIGHT TO BE HEARD.**

Responsibility for being heard

How much time, attention and space you can demand depends on you and the audience. The better you are at presenting the more of these you can claim. You not only have a right to be heard, you also have:

- **A responsibility for making sure you are heard.**

Some of us are good at blaming everyone and everything but ourselves, such as:

The audience was terrible
The Board have never liked me
No one wanted to hear what I had to say
Of course they were critical, they disagreed with me
There wasn't enough time
I didn't get a chance to prepare
Nobody wanted the truth anyway
There should have been a microphone
They hated hearing it from people at my level
I'd no time to make an impact
What can you expect just after lunch?

What's your favourite excuse for not presenting well?
    There is always something you can do to affect the situation.

- **Question yourself, before blaming the audience.**

Perfect Presentation comes through self-expression, presenting the essential you. When that happens you automatically make an impact. What commonly gets in the way?

OBSTACLES

Presenters often create self-made obstacles:

- Written notes
- Visual aids
- Body talk
- Sub-text
- Waffle

Written notes
Are you tempted to use full notes of everything you want to say? For some people it's reassuring to glance down at a full script. Yet full notes tend to trap you into reading them aloud. Few people can hold an audience that way. When you look down you must find your place, and the next step is to start reading. You may never return to the more important job of:

- **observing how your audience is receiving you.**

Read the section of Prompts (page 33) for more information.

Visual aids
When you are being yourself, sure of your message, committed to your presentation and closely in touch with your audience, using visual aids comes quite naturally. It's no longer a case of 'where shall I stand?' or 'how can I make the best use of the overhead projector?'

- If you worry about the technology, it's in the way.

Read the section on Presentation Aids (page 38) for more information.

Body talk

Your body cannot keep a secret and in presentations can literally betray you by contradicting what you are saying. Even highly competent people can undermine their impact through being unaware of what their body is saying. Yet once you possess this awareness it is usually possible to direct your body more positively.

Two main ways to improve your body language are:

- Being committed to a presentation
- Obtaining feedback on what you are doing

One of the best ways to obtain factual feedback is through using video to watch yourself in action. A safe place for that is either at home or in a workshop. However video is no panacea. It also takes sharp, informed observation to spot often tiny clues of which your audience can be aware, even unconsciously. For example, you may keep touching your nose or mouth during your performance which in some situations can suggest you may not be entirely telling the truth.

Watch yourself in a mirror when you are practising. You will often catch some extraordinary mannerisms that had previously gone unnoticed.

Sub-text

It's not only your body that gives you away. People talk about 'reading between the lines' or being able to 'read your mind'. They really mean there's a sort of sixth sense that exists between a presenter and the audience.

What is being communicated **underneath** the words, sometimes speaks louder than what is said aloud. If you don't believe what you are saying, for example, it will probably reveal itself somehow.

See also the section on Purpose.

Waffle

Just because your audience can hear your voice it does not mean they also understand what you are saying.

• Keep what you say simple.

A speech is a solemn responsibility. A man who makes a bad thirty-minute speech wastes only half an hour of his own time. But he wastes one hundred hours of the audience's time – more than four days.

Perfect Presentations eliminate anything not essential to the points you are making. Watch for those complicated sentences which seem like a Russian doll with ever smaller ones inside them.

• When you've made your point . . . Full Stop!

BASIC PRINCIPLES CHECK LIST

• Being a Perfect Presenter is all about being yourself
• Good presenters always review:
	what is it that I'm **not** doing and
	what **else** might work better?
• You are responsible for making yourself heard
• Never blame your audience
• Common obstacles to Perfect Presentations are:
	Written notes
	Visual aids
	Body talk
	Sub-text
	Waffle
• If you have to worry about the technology it's in the way

- Improve your body language through
    Being committed to your presentation
    Obtaining feedback on what you are doing
- Nothing is as powerful as the truth
- Keep what you say simple
- When you've made your point . . . Full Stop!

CHAPTER 3

The Five Ps of Perfect Presentation

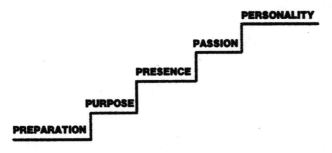

These five points are like steps on a ladder, covering just about every aspect of presentation and leading you towards becoming a Perfect Presenter.

PREPARATION

Preparation concerns everything about being ready for the delivery and includes:

- Research the audience
- Devise the presentation
- Organize presentation aids
- Check the venue
- Rehearse
- Ready yourself

PURPOSE

Presentations have objectives or aims. You expect certain results. There is often more than one purpose. You have an overall one which is the aim of the presentation, such as to have your report agreed, to explain a new product, or to achieve a decision.

Also within the presentation there may be many different purposes:

- Grab attention
- Explain who you are
- Establish credibility
- Make people smile or laugh
- Reassure them
- Alert them to something
- Make people angry, excited, pleased, concerned

PRESENCE

Presence is literally being present in the moment. It communicates a quality of aliveness, or 'being here' that commands attention. Everyone can possess presence. It is not confined to charismatic leaders or famous personalities.

You **can** increase your ability to convey presence.

PASSION

Passion is about caring. Choose any effective speaker or presenter and analyse why they are effective and at some level they really care about what they are saying.

Even boring material can be made interesting if your audience understands why you feel so strongly about it. They listen attentively because they sense you are saying something important. It is finding the human element of caring that makes the difference.

If you don't care strongly about your subject, why should your listeners?

PERSONALITY

Personality is bringing the whole of yourself into the presentation.

For example, some people are determined not to be nervous when presenting. They talk themselves into leaving their nerves outside the room. Sadly, they seem to leave some vital parts of their personality outside as well. The result is a bland information-giver, rather than *you*, who will make the difference.

These five stages are your route to success.

The rest of the book tells you more about these stages and how you can use them to improve your presentations.

PREPARATION

Careful preparation is when you:

1. RESEARCH THE AUDIENCE
2. DEVISE THE PRESENTATION
3. ORGANIZE PRESENTATION AIDS
4. CHECK THE VENUE
5. REHEARSE
6. READY YOURSELF

1. RESEARCH THE AUDIENCE

The whole point of presenting is to communicate, so:

• See it from *their* point of view

Put yourself in their shoes. It's fine having lots of ideas which you want to convey, but are they relevant? Is your audience going to understand you? Do they even want to? How much do you know about them? How many of them are there? You can probably think of many more questions.

The three starting points are: the audience, the audience and the audience. You may love or hate presenting, just never lose sight of your customers. That means being clear:

- Who am I talking to?
- How long can they spare?

For clarity on these, do your research on:

- Audience expectations
- Number attending
- Who talks before you
- Special factors

Most audiences have certain expectations. Even when you know your audience personally, it pays to review what they are expecting.

For instance, are they wanting to be persuaded, amused, informed, challenged to make a decision and so on? What's in it for them? Somewhere along the way the audience must get something they want or need.

To make an impact, you may deliberately choose to upset their expectations, but be sure to do it intentionally and not by mistake through ignorance or lack of preparation – it may even be useful to discover:

- How could I deliberately upset their expectations?

Check the level and background of the audience. What do you already know about the subject? Do they come already interested or must you generate the interest? Do they want to be there or have they been coerced? Are they fresh or already suffering from conference fatigue? Finally, most people have a set of personal values, prejudices or beliefs which influence how they receive communication. What are your audience's?

How many people will you be talking to? It's scary having prepared for a dozen people to find yourself facing two hundred. Clarifying the number helps you

- Judge audience knowledge
- Decide on appropriate presenting style
- Identify suitable presentation aids

What is big? Someone will speak of 'a large audience' when they mean a dozen people; to someone else it's hundreds or thousands.

- An audience of five to 10 people is a small group. You must establish relationships rapidly and try to engage each person, rather than just the group as a whole. You can sit, or perch on the edge of a desk if you prefer.
- An audience of 10 to 30 requires a more formal approach, though you will still be concerned with individuals. Visual aids need to be large and how you handle questions should be carefully considered. You'd do better standing up.
- From 30 to 100 the audience appears a mass of people, more anonymous and less easy to approach. It's harder to establish relationships with individuals

and presentation aids need to be faultless. Consider using a microphone.

- Over 100 people and you are moving into a theatrical situation. Issues such as stage decor, lighting, and presentation aids require considerable care and attention; question and answer sessions can fail unless formalized.

Special factors

There may be special factors about your particular presentation to review, such as:

- Who presents before me?
- What are they likely to say?
- What presenting aids will they use?
- How will they leave the audience for my follow-on?
- How can I tailor my presentation to build on or anticipate their expected impact?

You may be told you have an exact number of minutes to perform. It seldom means you must stick to that; you need to judge how much of you the audience can take. The best performers leave their audience wanting more.

Different presenting situations have different ground rules. For instance, if you are invited to give an after-dinner speech the time allowed may be more flexible than say a presentation to a board of directors. Sometimes you can ask a small audience: 'How long have I got?'

Watch out for situations where your audience have been affected by some special situation. For example, if they have just arrived from abroad will they be suffering from fatigue? Or you may not get their full attention because of anxiety such as job losses, a take-over bid or whatever. Find a way to acknowledge these situations during your presentation.

Consider your own credibility. For example, if you arrive to give a presentation instead of someone else who had been expected, you may need to explain carefully what you can offer that is special. Simply apologizing for not being someone else is no way to be a Perfect Presenter.

2. DEVISE THE PRESENTATION

Devising your presentation should be a creative experience. Here's a way of approaching the process so that what you eventually say will have

P-O-W-E-R

- **P** for PRODUCE
- **O** for ORGANIZE
- **W** for WRITE
- **E** for EDIT
- **R** for REFINE

Produce
Perfect Presenters produce something worth saying.

- If you've nothing to say, don't start talking

It's weak to begin by admitting you have nothing to say. An audience is entitled to more respect. Anyway, in most presenting situations you most definitely do have something to say.

To produce something worth saying you need to give your audience a new angle, a new piece of information or an interesting way of seeing the topic. If you hit real difficulty in finding something to say,

- Start with one thing about which you feel strongly and build on that

To produce something interesting there's no need to rely on luck. Instead, start by amassing anything and everything you might need for the presentation, no matter how remotely connected to it.

- Ideas, articles, quotes, statistics, photographs, illustrations, references, contacts, information, anecdotes, props, objects

Don't try making sense of it yet. That is the next stage. **Just accumulate everything remotely to do with your topic.** Build it into a collection. Stuff it in a drawer, a file or a box.

Once you start collecting, the amount of material will both surprise and please you. It widens the scope of your presentation, triggering off new ideas which you never thought were relevant.

Look for

- Themes
- Images
- Metaphors
- Analogies
- Symbols

that might run through your entire presentation, or visual devices which might convey important information or different ways of thinking about what you want to say. Find these by looking in unusual places, by making strange or surprising connections – just be inventive.

- Producing what you want to say becomes easier when you are being stimulated by material and information, which may not even be directly related to your presentation topic. Sitting in a room by yourself facing a blank sheet of paper is hard enough. Make sure you are in good company by way of stimuli.

Organize
You have accumulated all sorts of material around your topic. Now it's time to sort it.

- Examine your collection to see what new connections you can make
- Group similar items, themes or topics in separate piles
- Look at the structures below; see if your thoughts and ideas can begin to follow one of them
- Start dividing your collated material into relevant sections. Instead of having a box file full of scraps of paper, you may now have four or five different files. You can begin to see some sort of shape emerging

Structure is important in your presentation so that you are not merely talking at random. While some people structure instinctively, as they actually speak, not everyone has that gift.

Use a framework which helps you communicate and meet deadlines. There are some structures which work in a wide variety of situations. The best known is:

- Tell 'em what you're going to tell 'em
- Tell 'em
- Tell 'em again what you've told 'em

Or think of your presentation as a story with a definite

- BEGINNING
- MIDDLE
- END

Another, more imaginative, way is to think of your presentation as a piece of theatre with three acts.

ACT 1 – SITUATION. You outline the reason for the presentation by describing the current situation.

ACT 2 – COMPLICATION. Like all good dramas, there is a conflict or problem that needs solving. You might want to describe how bad things could be if no action is taken.

ACT 3 – RESOLUTION. What's it going to take to create a 'happy ending'? Your proposals will suggest a way forward that can produce the drama you want.

Every presentation you make is unique, even when you repeat well-used material. The situation may change, the audience will be different and how you feel can vary.

Many audiences are now familiar with the 'Tell 'em' structure mentioned above and using it risks being too predictable. It is generally better to devise your own unusual way to order and present material.

For example you could deliver your message as:

- A TV show, using a strong opener, lots of breaks, key moments and audience involvement
- A symbolic journey with varying stops along the way
- An unfolding drama, complete with hero, heroine, villain and a denouement
- A form of quiz in which the various questions gradually lead to your key message
- A play-let to illustrate your core proposition
- A major news broadcast, with headlines, an anchor person and interviews
- A dialogue between different experts, a customer and a sales person, an alien and an earthling, historical figures, and so on
- A courtroom drama putting your idea on trial

Thinking about your presentation in this way can suggest audience-grabbing elements, perhaps a curtain-raising opener, or a theatrical climax.

Or use our Instant Speech Guide, tested in our training workshops and which many people have found helpful.

FIVE STEPS TO AN INSTANT SPEECH

STEP 1 GET ATTENTION

Introduce your presentation with a grabby opening

STEP 2 THIS MEANS YOU

Explain the relevance of your subject to your audience

STEP 3 CENTRAL MESSAGE

Follow with a general statement of your purpose

STEP 4 FOR EXAMPLE

Support it with two or three examples or illustrations, including personal relevance

STEP 5 CLOSE

End on a striking sentence summarizing your speech

Right at the start, whoever you are, your audience wants to know if it's worth listening. So how can you get their IMMEDIATE ATTENTION? A grabby opening can include:

- A short, dramatic or controversial point
- Humour
- Involving the audience in some way
- Use of a powerful presentation aid
- Producing a real object or person(s)
- Doing something dramatic, an unexpected action

Right at the end find a grabby finish. It could be a brief reference back to your basic message, something from the above list or any other ending you can invent that will leave them wanting more.

Research into human memory shows people only easily remember about seven things at a time. There's a good case for speeches of impact only making three key points. Certainly most people try to cram in too much.

- What are the three (up to seven) things you want the audience to know?

People break the rules all the time in presenting. The seven point rule is no exception, yet it usually pays to follow it.

Write
An important step in creating a presentation is a rough draft; it might even be on the back of an envelope.

- Don't get it right – get it written
- Start writing and carry on until it is finished!
- Don't stop to edit, just let it flow out of you. You'll re-write and re-structure later
- Give yourself the luxury of creating a messy, imperfect first attempt

Writing is the hardest way of earning a living, with the possible exception of wrestling alligators.
   Olin Miller

People often become stuck while devising a presentation, so prepare for 'stuckness' through any of these actions.

- Find colleagues willing to stimulate you with ideas and see you through the tough times
- Sleep on it; give your mind a problem at bed time – it's often solved by morning
- Keep at it; who said it was going to be easy anyway! Persevere until it's complete
- Stimulate yourself with your own work: read aloud what you've got so far, it always sounds different that way; re-read your research and ideas file
- Take the dog for a walk
- Work on something else. Choose something horrible and difficult. You'll soon hunger to return to writing the presentation!

- Counter any depression with inspiration – listen to some inspiring music or read some wonderful literature

Eventually, you'll have a first rough draft, something to work on. Bad as it may be, it's a good place to begin.

Edit
Start eliminating the inessentials, anything obstructing your essential message and your (up to) seven points.

Too little material? This usually means that you're taking too narrow a view of your task. You may also be underestimating how long it will take to convey your material. Having outlined what you intend to say, given your main message, used examples and made your concluding remarks, you'll probably hit the time-limit.

The commonest problem, though, is not too little but too much material. If necessary, divide your information into:

- **Must know**
- **Should know**
- **Nice to know**

Once you organize material into MUST KNOW type information you may find there is little scope or time to include the rest.

As a general rule, run your pen through every other word you have written; you have no idea what vigour it will give your style.
Sydney Smith

Jargon-busting

Are you a jargon junkie? Do you happily use words, phrases, letters, acronyms, references, even images not part of the everyday language of ordinary people? Jargon is a presentation killer.

Jargon is comforting, intimidating, and says you have special knowledge. By excluding anyone unfamiliar with your private language, it becomes almost a form of aggression.

You may not even realize how much jargon you use. So be willing to ask for some independent advice on your jargon rating.

- Jargon is the last refuge of the poor presenter
- Be wary of using jargon even when talking to people from the same speciality or area of interest
- To detect jargon, begin by compiling your own jargon-busting list, the top ten words and phrases that are special to your own field
- Find someone unfamiliar with your jargon who is willing to say 'I don't understand'
- Try giving your helper a whistle to blow every time they hear you using jargon! Or ask them to tap a drinking glass so that it 'dings' each time you hit a jargon patch

Refine

Refining continues right up until you deliver the presentation so:

- Keep using feedback from colleagues
- Continuously adapt your presentation with new ideas as you perfect your material

If you perform the same presentation regularly it's

essential to keep refining it, otherwise you become increasingly stale. That's why salesmen sound so false and bored if they must present a set text with little freedom to improvise and refine. Each performance should be better than the last. Refining continues before, during and after the performance.

- Each time you perform the presentation you receive vital new information

Some people don't have much to say, but you have to listen a long time to find out.

Prompts

Even the most experienced presenters find ways to discreetly prompt themselves when presenting. Rather than attempting to hide your prompts as if they are a guilty secret, just ensure that they do not distract the audience.

Almost anything can become a prompt if it reminds you of your intention and what you want to say. It could be:

- Index cards with key phrases, keywords and pictures
- A small notebook
- The full script
- Mind Map
- Copies of slides or overheads
- Physical objects
- A note on your cuff or wrist
- Large boards with key phrases
- Mechanical device like a teleprompt

Whatever you choose it should be easy to see, without straining. Avoid the trap of using your slides as prompts as this tends to invite you to stare at the screen, rather than maintain a relationship with your audience.

Abandon anything that stops you concentrating on building a rapport with your audience. Reading a presentation or constantly glancing at notes:

- Distracts you and the audience
- Signals lack of confidence
- Deadens your delivery style

If you talk at conferences the teleprompt makes this situation worse. Although you read the entire script while seeming to look straight at the audience it gives a false sense of security. The effect is frequently deadening.

We have worked with people to overcome this and perform well, but it takes a lot of practice.

- Avoid reading notes word for word

There are bound to be exceptions, for instance when you must read a document verbatim for legal reasons.

Even these situations don't mean you have to read aloud like a human tape recorder. Become suitably familiar with your material and you'll still be able to give parts of it without direct reference to the notes. That's better than droning on like an automaton.

If you **must** rely on a full script

- Prepare notes with double spacing and in bold type, to find your way around easily when speaking

If there are many pages which have to be constantly turned it can be distracting to both you and the audience

- When you learn your words by rote there's a danger that you are donning a strait-jacket. You wonder 'will I remember the words?' and can easily be unnerved if you fail to say some part perfectly

Written words are only expressions of thought or feelings, so instead

- Learn the thoughts behind the words
- Know the basic structure of what you want to say and the essential ideas

Tell the truth, and you'll have nothing to remember
   Mark Twain

Four effective prompts are:

- Key words, pictures, mind maps and logos

Key words reduce what you want to say to a manageable form. You may originally write your presentation in full then whittle it down. How exactly do you do that? Here are the steps you take:

Step 1   Draft your presentation either in full or in fairly full note form
Step 2   Say the full presentation aloud several times until certain key words begin to jump out at you
Step 3   Highlight or underline these key words or phrases
Step 4   Do more run-throughs aloud of your presentation and begin relying on the key words rather than the notes
Step 5   Gradually transfer the key words to numbered prompt cards, on one side only

Step 6   Continue practising the presentation aloud, further reducing the number of key words or phrases and cards; aim for just one or two small cards

Some experienced presenters simply write the key words on their cuff, the palm of their hand or other discreetly accessible places.

Mind maps depict your entire presentation visually. They show key ideas and the more important links between them.

Notes on cards or a written script suffer from being linear. They start at one point and move logically through to a close. While this is helpful it can also prevent you from being more spontaneous and flowing with the ideas as you talk.

Here is a simple mind map for a presentation on managing meetings.

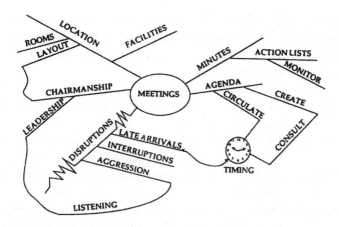

Build the Mind Map by starting with a single idea or theme in a circle, picture or any shape you want. Add lines and branches off them for the key ideas which you

write in capitals. Keep to single words if possible. Draw the linkages that occur to you or that you want to make in your presentation.

Use coloured highlighters to indicate ordering: for example, red for opening ideas, blue for the middle section and green for the closing portion.

When your whole presentation is shown as a bird's-eye view you can zoom down at will while still following a logical structure. The benefits become obvious when dealing with question and answer sessions. You can quickly relate each person's point to the relevant part of your mind map and deal with it in an interesting way.

Pictures and logos visually summarize your message and prompt key ideas rather than details. You don't need to be an artist to devise this kind of prompt. You're the only person going to see it anyway. Just create a simple drawing or symbol that encapsulates all or part of your message and use it as a prompt.

PREPARATION CHECK LIST

- Research your audience
- PRODUCE, ORGANIZE, WRITE, EDIT and REFINE your presentation – P-O-W-E-R
- Don't start talking if you've nothing to say
- To find what you need to say, start with something you feel strongly about, then build on it
- Amass ideas, articles, quotes, statistics, photographs, illustrations, references, contacts, information, anecdotes
- Look for themes; images; metaphors; analogies; symbols to run through your presentation
- Define the three (up to seven) things you want the audience to know

- Don't stop to edit, let it flow; re-write and restructure later
- Divide information into **nice** to know; **should** know; **must** know
- Learn the thoughts behind the words and the basic structure of what you want to say

3. ORGANIZE PRESENTATION AIDS

Presentation aids can help get your message across.

They can also confuse, bore, distract, overload and rob you of your impact. Use them with care and consideration, not from habit, or because everybody else uses them.

The gadgets and devices such as video, slides and microphones are the hardware. Your own specific material used in your presentation, such as a chart or video clip, is the software.

Hardware varies widely in complexity.

COMPLEXITY

LOW	MEDIUM	HIGH
Hand-outs, flip charts, display stands, white boards, and perhaps three-dimensional objects such as product displays.	Slide and overhead transparency projectors, simple sound systems and basic video playback.	Multi-slide and sound systems, on-line computer graphics projectors, high-image resolution large-screen projectors, laser pointers, teleprompts, wireless microphones, mobile displays and so on.

Whatever you use, it's worth including only when it gives you more

I-M-P-A-C-T

I	INTEGRATED into your style
M	MOVES the presentation on
P	PROFESSIONAL appearance
A	APPROPRIATE to the moment
C	COMMUNICATES to the audience
T	TECHNICALLY sound

Integrated into your style

You need to be comfortable with a particular presentation aid so that it becomes a natural part of your style. When you introduce a slide, flip chart, film clip, sound tape, overhead or whatever, it should be almost without thinking.

- An effective aid flows naturally from what you are doing

A particular presentation aid should not become a separate event. It should appear seamless within your performance.

When you enjoy using a particular visual aid it tends to communicate. The reverse is equally true. People quickly realize if you feel uneasy; for example, if you tend to worry that the technology might fail.

Do you feel compelled to use flip charts or overheads because everyone else does? If you find them cumbersome or cannot readily devise good ones, then do without; it won't enhance your performance to use a second-rate aid.

Every aid can go wrong. Flip charts can appear torn, dirty or too small. Slides can arrive upside-down, the film clip can break or the light on the overhead projector can fail mid-presentation.

When you feel you could sail through your presentation despite the worst happening, you are likely to handle it with confidence and make it part of your style. So:

- Assume the worst and prepare for it.

Move the presentation on
Presentation aids should only be used when they oil the wheels of your performance. Each aid must contribute to moving the presentation on – further than you could without it.

It's sometimes tempting to use a presentation aid which is powerful in its own right, such as a dramatic chart, a film clip or an amusing cartoon. This can reduce your overall impact unless it has a clear role in your developing presentation.

A visual aid which moves the presentation on leaves the audience glad that it has been used.

- Each aid should have a specific effect and purpose

Professional appearance
A professional-looking visual aid shows you respect your audience and says you are committed to making your communication succeed. 'Professional' means the quality of the material is at the highest possible level, consistent with your budget constraints.

Quality is always hard to define. Generally it means

- a pleasing appearance

- readability
- consistency of appearance, colour, size, and balance
- produced with care

Some of the principles of a professional appearance depend on sound graphic design. For example, eyes become distracted between visuals. So it's important to have titles all the same size, a standard print style and colours used consistently throughout.

This shouldn't however rule out home-made visuals, as long as they are carefully done. Some of the best are hand-drawn cartoons or symbols – they have a freshness and friendliness that can be very appealing.

Appropriate to the moment
The medium must suit your message and presenting situation. It may be inappropriate to show a film or slides to your board of directors, for example, unless they are warned and have the necessary time available. In some large organizations you wouldn't be considered effective as a presenter unless you used slides, or showed moving graphics.

However, the medium is appropriate only if it enhances your presentation. For example, despite its popularity the standard overhead projector is inadequate for most situations involving more than a few people unless it is to show only two or three transparencies.

Technology offers some exciting opportunities for making an impact. For instance you can project spreadsheets and graphics from a computer directly on to a screen. Computer-generated slides can actually be constructed and shown even as you speak. Yet our basic principle of total readability and being appropriate for that particular situation still applies.

The impact you want also governs your choice of medium, for example:

- Full colour slides suggest that content is official and has authority
- Hand sketched aids imply openness and informality

Take risks and surprise your audience. For example, use cartoons, summarize basic principles on a small give-away card, produce an object instead of a picture of something or a 'prop' as a symbol or metaphor. Only do it if it seems appropriate; for instance in some situations cartoons would be considered frivolous.

It is often effective to use music or film to enhance your presentation when you are not speaking. For example, before you arrive to talk you could have music playing, or a video running of a relaxing scene. If you have a break in your presentation try playing some music or a video.

Think of the room as a whole. How can you take charge of it and make it yours in some way? Perhaps you could put up visuals or objects to create an atmosphere and enhance your particular message. Anything goes as long as it works in your favour.

Communicate to the audience

Simplicity is the great principle behind good visuals and, where possible, use colour – it wakes people up. If you have to read your visual aloud it probably isn't working well enough.

Graphic design is a specialist field and if possible get professional help. Even if you cannot afford it at least make your graphics meet the minimum requirements:

- Totally legible by everyone in the audience

- Neat and consistent in appearance
- Clear message or image that communicates instantly

Poor legibility is one of the most consistent failures of aids. Never simply reproduce typed pages from books, reports or spreadsheets.

Basic rules of visibility are:

- No more than about six lines per visual
- Text large enough for **everyone** at the back to see
- Lettering sizes

Up to 10 metres	**5mm**
From 10–15 metres	**10mm**
From 15–20 metres	**15mm**

Assume the most important member of your audience arrives late, sits at the back and is fairly short-sighted.

The power of a visual is that it's . . . visual! Words and numbers are not visuals merely because they are on a screen or flip-chart. Where possible use your natural creativity to turn them into symbols, drawings, pictures, cartoons, images, charts, graphs, photographs, flow charts and logos.

Technically sound

Visual aids are part of the mechanics of presenting and no matter how simple, need to be technically sound.

The more complex the gadgetry, the more attention

you must give to seeing it works faultlessly. If you use a video, for instance, what happens if the playback machine breaks or develops a fault? Even when you are presenting in a totally professional environment with technician support, take nothing for granted.

Individual visual aids – the software – may also cause problems. In preparing them, mistakes can sneak in – particularly if you are delegating the work to others.

During the presentation, slides can appear upside-own, reversed, in the wrong order, with gaps between them; or be the wrong set entirely. Video clips may be played starting at the wrong place, or be missing sound. Overhead transparencies can fail to fit on the machine or on to the screen and so on.

- With presentation aids prepare for the worst

Using presentation aids
Regular presenters often carry their own tool kit to avoid having to chase around looking for items when they arrive at a venue. Your tool kit might include:

- Masking tape
- Flip chart and stand
- Set of coloured markers
- BLU-Tack
- Stapler
- Set of small index cards
- Presentation check lists

When you are sure of what you want to say, you're confident and won't worry too much about actually using your presentation aids. Rules for using presentation aids tend to be confusing and one soon forgets them.

However, to make your use of presentation aids become second nature, you do need to practise and be familiar with how to get the best from them.

Since every sort of presentation hardware has its own demands for using effectively we cannot cover everything here. But here are some basic tips.

Flip Charts
Have enough paper, a spare pad and at least three new coloured markers
Check stand for stability
Pre-score pages to be torn off
Lightly pencil in headings or drawings in advance
Write notes lightly in pencil in top corner
For locating a page quickly add a marked tab
For fast access to a page cut corner off previous one
Write REALLY BIG
Leave each page up for at least one minute
Don't leave a sheet up once you've moved on
Stand at the side or well clear of the page

Overhead Projectors
Have projector at 90 degree angle to screen or use angled screens to avoid distortion
Make sure lens and surface are clean
Locate where everyone can see
Make picture as big as possible
Use pre-drawn transparencies if possible
Frame transparencies, so they don't curl up with the heat
Avoid normal printed text on a transparency
Put each transparency on straight
Number all transparencies
Check pen(s) writes clearly
Turn off projector when not referring to a transparency

Have a spare bulb and know how to fit it
Covering parts of a transparency lets you reveal material
and focuses audience on only one point at a time
When finished, move projector right out of your way

Slide projector
Make picture as big as possible
Requires dim lights – may diminish your impact
Know which light switches to work and who'll do it
Number all slides clearly
Check slide order, and how placed in carousel
Have at least two run throughs on location
Perfect controls so slides all appear in right order
Make sure an assistant knows the cues for moving on
slides
Turn off projector and adjust lights immediately after
slides finish

Video
Use only if picture is large enough for everyone to see
Lights need to dim – may detract from your personal
impact
Know which light switches to work and who'll do it
Check each tape is positioned to start where needed
Know how to handle any remote controller and the TV
Number video tapes
List index location of start and finish of each clip
Turn off TV the moment you have finished with clip
Keep clip brief – your audience wants to see you, not a
film
Allow time for your audience to switch their attention
back to you after a clip
Don't leave the audience puzzled – tell them the source
of the clip
Avoid talking over a clip – instead freeze picture

Use effects like freeze-frame and slow motion sparingly
Don't let clips come between you and your audience
Can be a good attention grabber at start or a powerful
finisher

Portable projectors – computer connected
Allow plenty of time to resolve technical problem of get-
ting your presentation up and running
Start and end the sequence of images without a glaring
white blank screen – using the lens cap can do it simply!
Become adept at switching back and forth between visu-
als without fuss or delay
With a portable mouse, test constraints on distance or
location from the computer
Use the digital zoom facility sparingly

PRESENTATION AIDS CHECK LIST

- Use presentation aids only if you feel comfortable
  with them
- All presentation aids must have I-M-P-A-C-T!
- Be creative – use props, posters, music, mobiles,
  movement etc.
- Be clear about the specific effect each aid achieves
- Standardize on print style and keep it horizontal
- Make each visual aid totally readable by the furthest
  member of the audience, and make sure audio sys-
  tems can be heard by everybody
- Each visual should be connected logically to that
  particular point in the presentation
- No more than six lines per visual – often much less
- Only three major points to be made per page/slide/
  chart etc
- Keep visuals simple – tell audience how much infor-

mation they need to retain, and give them time to absorb the visual

4. CHECK THE VENUE

You are important and need showing off.

Your surroundings help or hinder what you say. For example, we have seen senior executives lecturing staff on total quality control while standing on a dirty platform and dressed in rumpled suits.

Whether you are presenting to a handful of people in an office, or to thousands in a conference hall, take the environment into account.

Professional presentations use set designers who make sure that the performer appears to best advantage. Clever designers balance the visual impact of the set with the impact of the performer. If you cannot afford such help you can still take responsibility for making the best of your venue.

The room
Your presentation starts from the moment people walk into the room. What is the first impression: does it make you feel comfortable, stimulated, repulsed?

What would make the place immediately more interesting and welcoming? It may not take much, perhaps just a neatly drawn flip chart saying WELCOME! or some other friendly devices such as quotes around the wall, illustrations or even objects.

Make the environment complement rather than undermine you. For example your performance may be wasted if the audience's attention keeps obsessively returning to a smudge on the wall by your right ear or waiting for the creak of a loose floor board, or catching sight of a flickering bulb.

You are vulnerable to becoming a victim to all kinds of environmental catastrophes such as:

- The sound system breaking down
- Electricity blackouts
- Fire alarms being tested
- Actual fires
- Hammering in the next room
- People collapsing, fainting, having coughing fits
- A rock group rehearsing next door
- A drunk in from the streets, or the board room!
- Audio visual gear missing or failing
- Doors slamming with every late-comer
- Add your own nightmare here

While you cannot anticipate everything you can take responsibility for running a basic check list of venue items past your host. At least give yourself a chance of dealing with some of the commoner events that undermine Perfect Presentations.

For example, you **can** do something about chairs that squeak and many other environmental factors.

- Visit the presentation room a day before, and again at least half an hour before you perform

Sit in a chair in various parts of the room or auditorium. Sit where you will be presenting. Being at a board table, for example, feels different to having nothing between you and the audience. Gain a sense of what it will be like for them and how it will feel being where you are.

In a room you continually use for some other purpose, like a canteen or a showroom, you may be battling against people's habitual expectations of it.

- How can you change the environment creatively, by re-setting the scene for your important message?

The above applies to the conference hall – only ten times more. Review the check list at the end of this section for more detailed hints.

If refreshments are to be served, do you know exactly when? Picture the scene. You are just about to hit the audience with the most important part of your presentation when . . . bang! The doors open and in march 20 waiters bearing trays of canapés! Or you are at a team presentation and in comes a conscientious tea lady anxious to sort out who is having tea, who wants coffee and anyone for buns?

Take responsibility for insisting the refreshments come at a suitable pre-determined moment before, during or after you present.

- Never be overpowered or surprised by caterers

CONFERENCE CHECK LIST

- Visit the room for the presentation a day before, and half an hour before you perform
- If necessary, change the environment creatively, by re-setting the scene for your important message
- If possible, see somebody else performing in the space beforehand
- Check the room's temperature, lighting, outside noise
- Are the chairs comfortable, with enough space between them and placed as you want them?
- Stand on a stage to get a 'feel' for it; how will you

have to project yourself to be heard? Will you sit or stand during the presentation?
- Practise speaking to experience the acoustics; have a colleague sit out front trying different seats to find out how you sound
- If you intend using a microphone and moving around, check the length of the lead, and make sure you won't fall foul of any creaking floorboards
- Ask people who know the environment to tell you of any local quirks
- CHECK AND DOUBLE CHECK THE VENUE!

5. REHEARSE

Rehearsing helps you to:

- Learn your presentation
- Become free to concentrate on the audience

If each time you drove a car you had to think how to steer or change gear you'd drive no more than a hundred yards. Certain actions must become automatic, leaving you free to watch other vehicles, people crossing the road and traffic lights.

The same applies to presentations. You must be free to build a relationship with your audience. Regardless of research or preparation there is much you cannot plan. So by mastering your presentation you give yourself room to relate to your environment and the audience – to be yourself.

Will rehearsing kill your spontaneity? While you can overdo it, most people do far too little, rather than too much. Actors rehearse long hours, why should **you** be able to talk powerfully to an audience with little or no practice?

- The best presenters take their rehearsing seriously

It usually takes me more than three weeks to prepare a good spontaneous speech
 Mark Twain

As Mark Twain implies, even ad libbing demands practice. Oscar Wilde was known to practise his apparently unrehearsed *bon mots* for weeks before he used them.

 Some ways you can practise are:

Devise the presentation
Practise in your head
Say it out loud
Do it in front of the mirror
Use a cassette recorder or video
Try it in front of other people
Rehearse it on site
Do it in front of the dog

Devising your presentation helps the information sink into the subconscious. Thus it's easier to master what you write than somebody else's speech.

 If you originally wrote a full script of your presentation, practice helps reduce it to key words.

 Practise on other people. Start small; ask just one person to hear you. Give clear instructions such as:

- Listen right through: don't stop me in mid-flow
- If you think of a way I might improve, write it down
- Note down anything that isn't clear

- What is in my main message?
- What feelings does my performance arouse?
- Tell me anything you'd like to hear more about

Everybody differs in how much practice they need. While you are the best judge of what you require, a general guide is:

- For each minute of talking spend 30 minutes rehearsing, perhaps more.
- Do it **as if** the audience were really there

Go over the top when rehearsing. Put more energy into it than on the actual day and use all the gestures. Exaggerate body movements, be louder and freer to emphasize key words and phrases. Gain a feel for what you are really saying through making your body experience the presentation, not just your mind.

Having been over the top a few times, you can always come back down again. It's far harder to go the other way and belatedly attempt to inject more energy and power into what you are doing.

Through rehearsal, the presentation becomes part of you. You know the ideas, the structure and the main message, not merely the words. It's no longer a job to be done; once inside you, it's a resource you can rely on.

Video can be a big help in noticing all kinds of things which you miss when just looking in a mirror. If you cannot use video try using a tape recorder to hear what the presentation sounds like. But there's no substitute for doing it live in front of another human being.

REHEARSAL CHECK LIST

- Practise where you will be presenting
- Devise your presentation yourself to make it memorable
- Rehearse until it becomes second nature, and you are free to concentrate on the audience
- Run through the presentation repeatedly in your head
- Say it aloud wherever you find yourself alone
- Rehearse using more energy than on the actual day
- See what you look like doing it, using a mirror or video
- Practise in front of other people
- Seek feedback and direction

6. READY YOURSELF

Perfect Presenters never start a presentation without ensuring that the equipment works. Yet the most important piece of presentation equipment is: YOU.

You deserve more care and attention than the physical equipment and also require regular overhaul! Develop a routine for preparing yourself before a presentation. It can help you get consistency in the quality of your approach. Just as golfers have a ritual before 'addressing the ball', so presenters can benefit from a pre-performance routine.

You have both **external** and **internal** resources to prepare yourself so let's look at these in action.

External resources consist of:

- VOICE – SPEECH – APPEARANCE – PHYSICALITY – STATURE

Voice

Even when using a microphone, you still need more vocal energy than for everyday speech. You can seldom rely entirely on a quiet conversational voice. Without a mike in front of a large group you will need to be LOUD.

Because your ears are only a few inches away from your mouth, sounds seem louder than for everyone else. To you it may seem like shouting, but to the audience it's perhaps barely audible.

Audiences are usually too polite to say they can't hear. It is possible to give a complete presentation, be hardly heard yet never know it.

* It's your responsibility to make yourself heard

An audience hates having to strain to hear. *You* should be doing the hard work, not them. So before you start, warm up your voice with exercises like saying some 'tongue twisters' or singing along with a tape in the car.

Some people naturally speak quietly and find it hard to believe how much they must increase their volume to reach an audience. If you are one of these, you may be unsure how to make your voice louder.

Your lungs are your volume control. So, the secret is . . . breathing!

Try this when you are alone.

STEP 1   Take a deep breath and make the air fill you right up, as if starting from your navel and piling up to your throat

STEP 2   Do it several times, get a feel for what being filled with air is really like

STEP 3   When you are filled with air say HELLO as loudly as you can. Let the air shoot out from you, carrying the word to the other side of the room

STEP 4   Now try it again, this time even louder

STEP 5   Practise saying several words and then several sentences by shooting them out from you when you are completely filled with air. This is how to sound louder without also sounding as if you are shouting.

Accents

Nowadays regional accents can give colour and flavour to a presentation, as long as you are intelligible. It also helps if you really appreciate the attractiveness of your own accent. It's worth checking whether:

- You can be understood
- You need to speak more slowly or carefully, articulating certain words
- There are suspect words your audience might not understand

Difficult Phrases

When you have a particularly tricky word or phrase to say, spend time becoming familiar with it. On our courses we have met

Globalized free flow of funds

Automatic axial-leaded insertion components

and many more.

These are taxing combinations and should be treated with respect. Just before your performance, ready yourself for any hard words or phrases by repeating them aloud. Professionals would say them slowly at first, and then more quickly until their mouths were performing efficiently.

Appearance

It is essential to check your personal appearance before delivering your presentation. You are your own visual aid and your appearance should complement your message.

For more details on this point, see the section on PERSONALITY.

Physicality

Breathing correctly is particularly important for Perfect Presentations because it helps to:

- Relax your body
- Eliminate tension
- Slow you down
- Quell panic
- Create and channel energy
- Give you and the audience space

So before you start your readying routine . . . BREATHE! Take at least three deep breaths.

How can you be a Perfect Presenter if you are crippled with tension? Use relaxation exercises to notice areas of tension in your body, and gently let go.

Use the mirror to check how you stand. See what it's like to spread your weight equally on each foot, to hold yourself upright and yet comfortable.

Mentally picture yourself as even taller than you are. Hold yourself fully upright as someone worthy of the time and attention which people are going to give you.

Your audience cannot easily relax and listen if you enter with an apologetic air, as if you wanted to be somewhere else.

Wondering what to do with your hands? These are expressive and a gift for communicating. When you fully express yourself, hands naturally lend emphasis. When you worry about them so does the audience.

- The performing energy that flows when you speak wants to animate your hands – let it

Hands were designed to hang from the shoulders and simply be there – ready to gesture on your behalf. If you feel more comfortable holding them together or one of them in your pocket, do so. Perfect Presenters find a comfortable place for their hands and leave them alone.

- Watch in case your hands become stuck in one position, locked into pockets, gripping a table, or grasping behind the back

Internal resources consist of:

- EXPERIENCE – ENERGY – FEELINGS – STYLE – PERSONALITY – PSYCHE

All of them help you become ready for the actual presentation, so be willing to draw on them.

Make a list of helpful reminders about how you want to be during your presentation. You can call them up before and during a presentation session. Examples other people have adopted include:

> Be a star
> Breathe
> Check the equipment
> Check flies
> Clarity not clutter
> Contact people
> Express my passion
> I can and I will
> Leave space
> Look up
> Smile more
> Pauses

A smile increases your face value

Put your most important reminder where you can see it during a presentation. For example, at the top of your script or notes you might write in large letters **BREATHE**. (Or have a picture of a smiling face).

Perfect Presentations require more energy than chatting to your neighbour at the next desk.

- To warm up your voice and body use some vigorous body movements to get the energy flowing.

Do this in private or people may think you rather strange, jumping up and down or waggling your hands violently!

Closely linked with energy are your feelings. Emotions are an amazing resource and are usually the key to making a real impact. Perfect presentations move audiences in some way. They get excited, inspired, enraged, challenged, satisfied, entertained – you name it. These are feelings and there is nothing reasonable about them.

Once you know what feelings you want to communicate you can use this to help ready yourself for making an impact.

For example, if you are going to tell people about an exciting new project, then make sure you too are excited before the presentation. Your own feelings not only affect your performance, they influence the audience too.

To re-connect with feelings about how you want to be during the presentation you may find that one phrase, sentence or image captures your feelings about the issue or about your personal style. Keep repeating it to yourself. As you breathe, you will probably find the mere repetition of the key phrases gets your feelings going.

Choose a special reminder to yourself which captures your desired feeling or personal style; it could be a saying, jingle, aphorism, or catch-phrase.

Real examples from our workshops are:

I'm the truth-teller
Peter the powerful
Nice'n easy does it every time
Hit 'em between the eyes
Big, bold and bouncy
All the time in the world

What will your personal style slogan be?

Stage fright

Absolutely everybody, including the Perfect Presenter, is nervous before presenting. Something important is about to happen (if not, don't bother to present – send a report instead!).

When important events occur, your body knows you are being risky. Adrenalin rushes around your system providing a wonderful source of energy and excitement. However, we often panic when that happens, which feels uncomfortable, even unpleasant.

Instead, breathe gently and deeply. Allow the symptoms to exist and observe them, reminding yourself that you would feel the same if you were excited. You *are* excited! Of course you are: something important is going to happen.

Create a picture of the energy flowing through your body and enjoy it. Welcome it as a friend, a power to harness and channel into your performance. When you accept it, the uncomfortable feelings will cease to matter.

All this is rather easier said than done, of course, which is why workshops and courses can provide you with a safe environment in which to practise handling these feelings.

• Keep imagining your presentation going well

In our workshops we provide a cassette with a visualization for building your confidence. (Drop us a line if you would like one). You can develop your own version in which you run a film through your head and 'see' yourself giving the Perfect Presentation. The more times you run the film through your head, the more impact it has on the real event.

Finally a useful way to handle stage fright is, early on, to get the audience working in some way. You can ask them to give a show of hands, get them talking in pairs, ask them to introduce themselves. Once the attention is switched to the audience in this way you will find your stage fright is much reduced.

Everyone has butterflies – it's the professional who gets them to fly in formation

PREPARATION CHECK LIST

- It's your responsibility to make yourself heard
- Establish a preparation routine before presentations
- Try singing alone with a tape in the car on your way to the presentation. Or do some long 'Aaah' sounds
- Spend time practising tricky words or phrases
- Before you start your readying routine . . . BREATHE! Take at least three deep breaths
- Check that your appearance doesn't distract from your message
- The performing energy that flows when you speak wants to animate your hands – let it. Otherwise, find a comfortable place for your hands and leave them alone
- Make a list of helpful reminders to use regularly before any presentation and place these where you can see them
- Develop a personal style slogan
- Deal with stage fright by observing the feelings and reminding yourself you are excited; let the energy flow through your body, channelling it into your performance – and above all BREATHE!
- Keep imagining your presentation going well

PURPOSE . . . IN PERFORMANCE

Apart from the general purpose of your presentation you also have a purpose during each moment of the performance.

So many presentations appear flabby, undynamic and pointless because this crucial aspect has been overlooked. When you are presenting you are not in a world of your own. Quite the opposite. Presentations are about relationships. You are building several relationships all at the same time. And these involve some sort of action or response from your audience. You are talking to them in order to have an effect on them. Even if they appear passive, they are not. At every moment, they are experiencing all sorts of feelings. If they're not experiencing what you intend, what *are* they feeling?

Addressing the issue of purpose, forces attention on where it matters – your audience. Since you continually have an effect on them, it helps if it is the effect you want.

Nail down what is behind each part of the presentation. If you can't be sure . . . cut it out!

Ask yourself:

- Why am I telling them this – now?
- Why am I doing this – now?
- What effect do I want to have?
- What result do I wish to achieve?
- What should be different by the end of this presentation?

For example, suppose you intend saying: 'We make the finest fire-resistant glass doors in the country.' Checking your purpose reminds you the sentence is there because you want to **impress** your audience. You would deliver such a sentence differently if instead you merely wished to **reassure** them. Try it. Say the sentences as if to impress someone and then as if to reassure them – sounds different doesn't it?

By reducing your purpose down to a single phrase or key word, like impress, excite, involve, shock, amuse, you are forced to be far more specific about your presentation than just its topic or title.

For instance, if you are giving an after-dinner speech, is your purpose: to amuse; to inform; to thank; to arouse; to lull and so on? Which parts are meant to do what – do you know, or are you merely hoping?

Once you've decided your purpose it can fundamentally influence how you approach your performance. When you have a written reminder note of these key purposes, it could prove to be all you need instead of detailed notes.

Variation

Changing your purpose also provides variation of tempo, attack and intonation. Think of it as a journey – taking your audience on a trip through changing countryside, winding and bumpy roads, varied outlooks. Sometimes you're speeding ahead, other times lingering to enjoy the view. You keep changing gear. A journey like this is more exciting than cruising on a dreary motorway. Your presentation should have a similar variety, which comes from constantly changing and developing the purpose.

Think of a presentation as a two-way conversation in which we only hear one side. You could even structure your entire presentation around imaginary questions from your audience. Consider what they will want to know. For instance you may well have decided to open your speech with a brief description of your background and experience. The purpose of this is to – 'establish your credibility'. Why not do it in response to an imaginary question from the audience. In your mind, select somebody and imagine they've asked you the question 'what qualifies you to talk about this topic?' Then answer the question. This helps you remain permanently in touch with your audience and strengthens your sense of purpose.

If possible allow real questions from your audience since again, if your purpose is clear, you can handle anything that comes up.

Handling Questions
Questions are a perfect opportunity for you to achieve your overall purpose. They allow you to expound on your ideas and make them relevant for your audience. However, notice how you handle them. For example, if your overall purpose is 'to win over', 'to achieve a commitment' or 'to inspire', then you are unlikely to succeed by answering questions with an attitude that says: 'put down', 'complete' or 'lecture'.

This is particularly tricky when facing hostile questions. The purpose of these is often 'to catch you out' or 'show you up'. Your instinctive reaction might be to retaliate. Instead, your real intention is to 'persuade them' or 'get them on your side'. So answer the questions appropriately.

PURPOSE CHECK LIST

- Be absolutely sure about your purpose
- Sum it up in a single sentence
- Know why you're telling them this – now
- Clarify 'what result I want to achieve'
- Define 'what effect do I want to have?'
- Identify 'what should be different after the presentation'
- Aim to establish a relationship with your audience
- Think of a presentation as a two-way conversation in which we only hear one side
- If possible, allow real questions from your audience

PRESENCE

Effective presenters establish a presence with an audience. What is it and can you do it too?

Presence is literally showing your listeners you are really 'present' in that particular moment. It creates in their minds an acute awareness of your existence so they become alert to what you do next.

You also become alert to all that is happening around you. Your own awareness heightens that of your audience who become acutely receptive to your communication.

Try it now. In a moment put this book down and do the exercises below to become more alert to what is going on right now.

Let each sense absorb the information as you place your attention on it.

Presence Exercise
SIGHT
Look around you carefully and slowly.

See anything you have not noticed before? Look at the details. See the colours. Imagine that you have a tele-photo lens and can zoom in on certain tiny things. Now use a wide-angle lens, take in the whole panorama.

HEARING
Close your eyes and listen. It takes a few moments to hear all the sounds around you, but soon you'll wonder why you did not hear that clock ticking in the first place, or that computer hum, that clicking of train wheels and so on.

SMELL
What can you smell right now? Take a few gentle, slow intakes of breath and discover whether you can scent

anything around you. Smell your own skin and clothes. If possible open a window and smell the air outside.

TOUCH

Touch is experienced all over our body, not just through our hands. Can you feel your clothes against your skin, the chair beneath you? Let your hands touch different things around you. Feel the varying textures and temperatures of different objects.

With your eyes closed bring your hands together gently until they touch. Do it again, try to feel the heat of each palm just as it is about to touch the other hand. How near can you get without touching?

TASTE

What is the taste in your mouth right now? Open your mouth and take a breath. Can you taste the air?

Becoming more aware in this way you acquire essential information about what is happening around you. You develop a heightened sense of alertness to the situation and its potential.

This alertness is a fundamental component of PRESENCE and it's what helps make Perfect Presenters. You can have the best script, know all your words, handle your visuals faultlessly yet you will not give an exceptional presentation unless you can create a presence.

We all have the potential to use our presenting skills to establish a presence; it is not the exclusive preserve of famous TV figures or great leaders. The alertness which presence creates is a form of chemistry, creating a two-way reaction between you and the audience. It can feel strange because it demands a blend of intuition and your ability to reason.

If logical reasoning alone was sufficient, many highly talented people would have a powerful presence. And if only intuition mattered, many creative and sensitive individuals would automatically convey it.

Some people are stronger on either logical reasoning or intuition and it is the combination of these two powers that works best.

When you establish a presence, that moment in time, however long it lasts, is your moment. It is a time when you are indisputably centre stage, commanding attention, alert and alerting.

In that moment you are positively aware of life as it is happening – moment to moment. It feels real. You are there, without any of the masks which we so often feel obliged to wear in challenging situations. Honest and vulnerable. You feel truly yourself.

Although you can practise to achieve presence, you cannot do it as a trick. Presence may not be worn as a mask since people merely see someone putting on a front. It has to be honest. And when it is, it has its own quality of commanding power.

You have a right to command such attention. Every human being does. You are entitled to be heard, seen, noticed, respected and acknowledged. When you are claiming that right, presence has three separate phases: establishing; maintaining; and ending.

Establishing
While each person must ultimately find their own special way of creating a presence, a basic approach which proves to be effective in many different situations is 'The Presenter's Highway Code':

STOP!

BREATHE

LOOK

LISTEN

FEEL

Your presentation begins by taking all these actions, usually before you have uttered a word. In meetings or small gatherings where you are not formally making a presentation these actions might occur after an opening sentence requesting people's attention because you have something to say.

Stop!
Before starting your presentation you STOP!

Though people are expecting you to speak, instead you pause, taking stock of the moment. It is a delicious, exciting, risky and ultimately rewarding moment when you are, in effect, 'arriving'.

Inside you are taking time to settle down and adjust to being there, savouring the moment. During it you are making space to contact yourself and your audience.

The value of STOP! is that it prevents you rushing into your presentation as if you cannot wait to finish. Perhaps that is how part of you feels. But when you Perform With Presence this feeling is converted to a more positive energy.

STOP! also allows your audience time to adjust to your arrival centre stage.

Breathe
Having given yourself a moment to arrive how do you use it?

Take a deep breath, without heaving your chest or raising your shoulders. Draw in a lungful of breath and let it out gently, until all the air is expended. Think of yourself as a tube of toothpaste squeezing out as much paste as possible, until there is none left.

If it's appropriate, do this several times. It has an automatically calming effect on the body and mind.

Breathing in this way is the secret of many good presenters. They do it at the beginning of their performance and at appropriate moments during their presentation.

Try the following breathing task.

Breathing Task

Step 1   Place yourself in a comfortable position, either in a chair, standing up or lying down flat with your head slightly raised by a couple of books.

Step 2   Open your lips very slightly, just enough to allow the air to flow out easily.

Step 3   Expel the air from your lungs gradually, without rushing it (imagine you're making a candle flame flicker, but not blow out). When there seems no more air to push out pause for a few seconds before beginning to inhale. If it helps count to five before inhaling.

Step 4   Close your lips. Inhale your next lungful of air through your nose. Do so gently, without sounding as if you are giving a long sniff.

Step 5   When you have filled your lungs fully again pause a few seconds before once more opening your lips to let out the air.

Practise taking five or six breaths this way and then focus on reviewing how you are feeling. You should be experiencing a sense of calm and peace. If not, practise a little longer and it will certainly come.

Look

Having stopped and breathed now look around and take note of your surroundings. This is an opportunity to make a real contact with your audience and vice versa.

In a small group you can make eye contact with each person, just briefly before moving on. In a larger audience you may not be able to make individual eye contact with everyone. Do so though to one or two people, perhaps when you see a familiar face or someone appearing to smile at you.

While you are looking you are also observing your environment. Move your head around as well as your eyes. Notice the way people are sitting, that someone is shuffling some papers and not yet looking at you, that there is a bright light coming from one of the windows and so on.

Looking around takes command of the situation. It is an assertive act to which your audience will respond, perhaps many of them unconsciously.

You may find it helps to ask yourself:

'What do I observe right now?'

Hear the answers in your head as you continue looking around.

Listen

Similarly, take time to listen as you look around. You may notice the sound of the air conditioning, or of a police car with its siren sounding, that several people are coughing or blowing their noses, or shuffling their feet.

Listening tells you precisely the right moment to start your presentation. You can listen for that special moment when everything seems ready for your energy and contribution.

Feel

Lastly, take stock of how you are feeling that moment. What is your body doing, which parts are tense or relaxed, are your hands sweaty, is your jaw tight, what is happening in your solar plexus and so on.

If you are someone who suffers from stage fright this pause to review how you are feeling is extremely helpful. Instead of trying to push your anxiety away and forget it, you acknowledge its existence.

By accepting you are slightly tense or anxious, you can convert this feeling into a positive form of energy which gives your presentation more power.

Ask yourself:

'How am I feeling right now?'

Putting it all together

How long does it take to Stop! Breathe, Look, Listen and Feel?

As long as necessary. It is an unhurried process that each person uses in their own particular way. It certainly takes longer to describe than to do.

When you become used to these various activities you will willingly extend the time spent on them even if it seems a little risky in making your audience wait for your opening remarks.

Having used the Stop! Breathe, Look, Listen and Feel process to establish yourself, you begin your presentation.

Maintaining a Presence

Once you are under way how can you maintain the presence you have established?

This depends on your

• Presentation content

- Energy output
- Continued alertness
- Personality

The presentation itself plays an important part in keeping your hold over the audience. The preparation work which you did in the earlier stages can now produce results.

Energy output
Every effective presenter broadcasts a certain amount of energy which is picked up and used by the audience. By energy we do not mean some mysterious, metaphysical quality, but the vigour and dynamism of how you behave.

The longer the presentation the more you must sustain the energy level to hold your audience's attention. If you wind down so will the audience.

Raise energy levels during your presentation by giving each sentence and paragraph a renewed impetus. Seek ways to vary your

- Quality of expression
- Loudness of voice
- Face and body language
- Timing

In the section on Purpose, we looked at how to achieve variety in a presentation by continually changing the effect you wish to have on your audience.

You can produce different effects by altering the expression with which you deliver your words. For example you can vary the amount of seriousness used at different stages of the performance.

By deliberately adopting different tones and loudness an audience can be kept alert and interested in what is coming next. Many people are unaware that they are not regularly changing their voice to introduce variety. The result is either a monotone or bland and boring sound.

Loudness alone does not maintain presence. It requires a mixture of levels. As you change from one to another the audience should register the difference and feel stimulated.

It is said that the body cannot keep a secret and this is particularly true during a presentation. You cannot readily fake body language and expect to get away with it. We are all experts in body language. We grow up learning to read other people through their facial and body expressions and for example can usually tell when somebody does not like us or is bored in our company.

As you tackle different parts of your presentation your internal thoughts and feelings will change and you allow these to alter your face and body language. This helps to sustain your presence and makes the changes seem natural and flow from what you are doing.

Timing
Vary the timing of what you say to keep the audience on its toes, constantly wondering what will happen next.

If you have a tendency to speak quickly, choose parts of your presentation where you force yourself to go slowly, pause, wait for reactions and so on.

Or, if you are a rather slow speaker, pick certain parts of the delivery to be speeded up and use your natural slowness to achieve an effect at appropriate moments. Perfect pace is listening speed. As such it is determined by your audience. They need time to assimilate your information. So leave plenty of space for *them* to do some work, while you have a chance to take a breath.

There is a tremendous amount you can do with timing to create an impact. For example, if you pose a question to an audience and then immediately answer it, you will have a different effect than if you wait several moments while they mentally try to answer it for you.

Variations in timing are like tunes: some are more attractive than others. The best way of learning about timing is by experimenting, to discover how a different pace or a variation in rhythm of speaking can affect the presentation.

Ending
Even if you have successfully held your audience you will eventually cease being centre stage. How can you do this effectively?

Finish your presentation in some memorable way that leaves both you and the audience on a high note. Never let your presentation drift into a vague ending.

You are responsible for making the end a positive one that hands back the centre stage to the audience or perhaps another speaker. You want to leave people feeling as they might at the end of a good meal. They put down their knife and fork feeling satisfied and complete.

The more definite you make the ending the clearer the audience will be about your intentions and appreciate this certainty. Once good presenters have finished they do not hog the limelight, they allow their impact to reverberate.

You can use the Stop! Breathe, Look, Listen and Feel steps at the end too. They can again help you avoid hurrying from the centre stage and instead leave it calmly and deliberately, enjoying the experience and learning afresh from it.

Spontaneity

Being present lets you react spontaneously to the situation. The more prepared you are, the greater your ability to ad-lib and deal with the unexpected.

If you have given the presentation countless times this is all the more reason to get 'present'. It will force you to speak as if it were the first time.

PRESENCE CHECK LIST

- Use the Highway Code of:

STOP!

BREATHE

LOOK

LISTEN

FEEL

- At the start take a few deep breaths, without heaving your chest or raising your shoulders – count slowly to 5
- Look around and note your surroundings; make contact with your audience and vice versa
- In a small group make eye contact with each person, just briefly before moving on
- With a large audience make eye contact with one or two people, look for a familiar face or someone appearing to smile at you
- At the start of your presentation ask yourself 'what do I observe right now?'; hear the answers in your

head as you continue looking around

- Take time to wait for that special moment when everything seems ready for your energy and contribution
- Keep up the energy levels and vary your:
      Quality of expression
      Loudness of voice
      Face and body language
      Timing
- End your presentation in some memorable way leaving both you and the audience on a high note.

PASSION

What does passion have to do with Perfect Presentations? Everything!

One always speaks badly when one has nothing to say.
  Voltaire

Passion can make or break your performance since powerful presentations connect with feelings, not just thoughts. Whether you are presenting to the boardroom or making an after-dinner speech, talking to a team or addressing a parent's association, passion is what touches them.

Passion in a presenter can warm, excite, enthuse, amaze, and interest because it reaches beyond our rational self. This may seem strange. Some people prefer dealing with facts, information, and analysis. Feelings are considered messy and hard to understand. Surely one can present well without resorting to passion?

No! Perfect Presentations always connect with feelings at some level. This doesn't mean your presentation must reduce the audience to tears, make it laugh hysterically or become angry. It is just that good presentations engage more than the ear; they capture the heart.

Good presentations create just the right level of emotional involvement for that particular audience. Don't be fooled by the idea that some audiences might not want any emotional involvement. For example, at a board meeting presenting accounts, or giving a report on a serious situation or telling a team some information.

If it requires you as a human being to communicate it, it also needs some passion somewhere. Being a powerful presenter means gauging both how to connect with feelings and at what level.

'But nothing really moves me!' you may say. In one sense that's true. If you refuse to make contact with what is going on inside then you will certainly remain unmoved. You are also in danger of becoming emotionally dead. Your audience will definitely notice.

An orator is a person who says what he thinks and feels what he says

Try one of the feelings exercises below to help you tackle this kind of problem.

Feelings exercises
Here are some exercises to increase your everyday awareness of your feelings, your interests, concerns and beliefs. Try them, however uncomfortable they seem at first.

1. Before you go to sleep at night, carefully review your day. Recall the events and examine how they made you feel.

You will soon enjoy the habit of looking for those

feelings and appreciate the increased self-awareness it brings.

2. Start a FEELINGS LOG

At the end of each day make a list (or circle) the feelings you have experienced. See which of these you experience.

GLAD	SAD	MAD	AFRAID
Happy	Unhappy	Angry	Nervous
Amused	Upset	Frustrated	Apprehensive
Delighted	Disappointed	Fed up	Terrified
Joyous	Let down	Annoyed	Fearful
Smiley	Lonely	Mingey	Wary
Content	Alone	Impatient	Guarded
Comfortable	Depressed	Bitchy	Secretive
Giggly	Low	Irritable	Threatened
Pleased	Run down	Reckless	Vulnerable
Excited	Miserable	Furious	Cautious
Sexy	Melancholic		
Courageous	Grieving		

Pick out the highlights at the end of the week and note them on the lines below. Do the same the next week and compare the results a week later.

YOUR OWN LIST: _____
_____
_____
_____
_____

Presentations are like a mirror, reflecting back what you are giving out. When you feel strongly, caring about your message, the audience too will respond at some emotional level. In one sense the audience must 'buy you' and your conviction.

At its simplest, if you don't care much about your message nor will your audience. To make an impact you will need to reach beyond the rational and connect at a deeper level. Otherwise just hand out the script and say 'read it'.

- **Feelings, not facts, move people**

The energy link
Passion is closely connected to energy. When you express strong feelings you both use and radiate energy. This is a gift to the audience and it usually responds.

'But how can I put passion into everything?' some people ask.

It gets easier the more aware you become of your everyday feelings – moment to moment. You can't treat passion like a tap, turned on only when you make a presentation. Do that and what comes out will be rusty, discoloured and unpleasant.

Much of our lives are spent totally unaware of our feelings. This makes it hard when we want to call on our anger about a cause or to be joyful about a success, or to make a powerful presentation.

Good presenters know why they care about what they are saying and also why the audience should care. They use their passion to energize themselves and the audience. The result is that their message is heard and people are persuaded, entertained, aroused or amused.

Passion is therefore an absolutely essential ingredient of the Perfect Presentation. Get this part right and just about everything tends to follow naturally. Put genuine conviction behind what you are saying and common worries like 'how should I stand, what shall I say, how shall I say it, what will they think, when should I stop,' will tend to take care of themselves.

Whatever your presentation is about there is always some part of it, however obscure, that connects with your passion. The challenge is to find that trigger point to drive your presentation forward and give it energy. After all, all facts and figures have a 'bottom line'. The bottom line is their importance.

Why do *you* think the figures are vital?

Why should the audience think they are vital?

Find this link and you will put a power into your performance as a presenter that will surprise you and perhaps your colleagues.

Focus your passion by converting strong feelings into a single sentence. For example

'If we don't all get together and commit ourselves to this strategy we're dead'
'I'm sick and tired of wasting this company's resources'
'It's the most fabulous opportunity we've ever had'
'It'll be a tragedy if they close this school'

Then you can go further and distil your key passion sentence into core expressive words such as:

Commit or we're dead
I'm sick and tired
It's fabulous
It'll be a tragedy

Once you've found some expressive words about your presentation, practise saying them aloud. Allow yourself to experience the feelings as you say them. Exaggerate the delivery so that you express them with more passion.

You may not express them with so much force in the actual presentation but you can use the emotions and insight to give your presentation real impact.

Passion means you speak about what's important to you. So what *is* important to you? Try the next exercise to find out.

Strong Feelings exercise

List six things about which you feel really strongly. Anything from politics to fishing, from bad driving to your previous boss.

I feel strongly about   *Rank order*

1. _____   _____

2. _____   _____

3. _____   _____

4. _____   _____

5. _____   _____

6. _____   _____

Rank these from most important (=1) to least important (=6).

Now start exploring the most important item by trying to relate it to your forthcoming presentation. Don't worry if the connection is tenuous and slightly absurd.

What ideas does this process of artificial connection trigger? Can you see any other interesting, unusual link-ages? Spend a few moments discovering what comes up.

Then do the same with the next most important item.

This is a form of brainstorming which you can do alone. It uses your strong feelings to help guide what you want to say and how to say it.

Personal Research exercise
You are the perfect source for discovering where your passion lies.

When you consider your life so far, what events have had most impact on you? Make a list of them and the associated feelings.

EXPERIENCE   FEELING

_____   _____
_____   _____
_____   _____
_____   _____
_____   _____
_____   _____

See if you can use these to improve your presenting.

Another way to contact your passions is to start making a record of situations, films, books, encounters, cultural events, news items, stories, and so on that move you.

Because they have made a strong impact on you they may anger or inspire you, threaten or enliven you.

Are there any common themes? For instance, you might discover that many of them are about the oppression of innocent people, or individuals surviving against all the odds, or people taking great risks or achieving great sports victories.

Doing this will certainly show what moves you. It will help suggest a source of your passion.

Being passionate is rather risky and definitely exciting. It's what makes presentations really worth doing.

Otherwise they are just the imparting of information, which is better communicated in written form, like a memo or report. Presentations are personal and should always involve some feelings.

Nothing great was ever achieved without enthusiasm
  Ralph Waldo Emerson

PASSION CHECK LIST

- Feelings, not facts, move people
- When you feel strongly about something you radiate energy
- Discover why you care about what you are saying
- Identify the key passions in your presentation
- Express key passions in a single sentence
- Why should the audience really care about what you are saying?
- If the presentation isn't going to make a dynamic impact – SEND A REPORT!

PERSONALITY

When some people mount the platform at a conference they leave their own personalities behind. Later they realize they could have made more impact. They did not do justice to themselves.

Or a manager speaking to employees wonders why, when given the chance, they never seem to ask questions or respond.

Perfect Presentations mean you are willing to use your

unique personality to make an impact. Simply by exerting your personality in a situation, you make a difference. Perhaps that's what Woody Allen meant when he said that 'ninety per cent of success in life, is turning up!'

Your personality makes your presentation different and therefore worth hearing. Never assume the facts speak for themselves – they don't. We are really asking

- How much of the real YOU comes through?'

Who do you think are good presenters?

Make a list of the ones you admire, not necessarily all famous. Pick people you feel communicate dynamically and make an impression.

PRESENTER   ATTRIBUTE

_____   _____
_____   _____
_____   _____
_____   _____
_____   _____

Against each name write the one personality attribute which most represents that person. It could be their humanity, humour, vigour, passion, enthusiasm, command of language and so on.

Look at your list and think about that person. You probably have a sense of who they are. They are distinguished because of their personality. They hardly waste much energy on trying to be like someone else – unless they make a living by impersonations! They are themselves. It's their uniqueness, their difference if you like, that makes them memorable and admirable.

They have become PERSONALITIES.

You too have your own personality and therefore

your own style of presenting. You may not be entirely clear as to what it is, or how it can be used to your advantage, but it is definitely there.

Every job is a self-portrait of the person who did it. Autograph your work with excellence.

It is time to develop your SELF-AWARENESS.

Make a list of the most important personal qualities which you believe you possess. Try to use single words like integrity, humour, drive, intelligence and so on.

_____	_____	_____
_____	_____	_____
_____	_____	_____
_____	_____	_____

Now ask a couple of people you know at work and two people who you know socially, to describe you. It will be interesting to see how others see you, compared with how you see yourself.

What qualities do people see in you socially but which are missing at work or when you give presentations?

Now see if you can write a description of yourself. For example, a reporter has been commissioned to write a profile article about you. After being interviewed, write the reporter's opening paragraph.

Use this information to develop further your picture of how you are coming across. The more you express your WHOLE self during your presentation the better you'll be and the better you'll feel about it afterwards.

Sometimes it's appropriate to express only a part of ourselves in certain situations. For instance, if you are announcing redundancies you would probably want to feature the part of you that is serious and compassionate. It is no time for frivolity.

In our workshops we help people begin to understand how they come across on first impressions. We use video and various exercises which break through the barriers people instinctively use to stop themselves seeing what they imagine may be unpleasant truths. Often, though, people are genuinely surprised that what comes across is different from their assumptions about themselves.

If you can attend a course where you have a chance to gain feedback of this kind, it will help you a great deal and you'll enjoy yourself into the bargain. Even without attending a workshop there's still plenty you can do to test how you come across as a personality.

You need to discover an important fact about yourself – who you are. We don't mean your name or job title, but what makes you, you. What is it that's so special about you? You definitely are special, you are unique!

What is it about you that particularly comes across when you communicate with people? Do they gain the impression that you are mainly serious, or jokey, in a hurry or usually thoughtful?

When you unravel how you are mainly seen by others it is enormously helpful to becoming a better presenter. In particular when you have checked out the general effect you have, you can then afford to do the opposite and not worry that you will go too far.

For example, suppose people mainly see you as coming across as jokey, always being amusing and seeing the funny side of life. Then during a presentation you can afford to give yourself permission to be serious and deliberately choose not to be jokey sometimes. The impact will be considerable yet people will not start seeing you as no longer jokey. You will have added another dimension to your personal expression.

Or suppose you tend to be a rather serious person and come across that way in presentations or communicating with people. Then during a presentation you can give yourself permission to be occasionally funny and jokey without worrying that people will think you are a frivolous person.

• Knowing how you come across initially, gives you permission to be the opposite.

Style

Another way of exploring your personal qualities is to review how you express yourself. What kind of language do you tend to use, do you use jargon, do you like using certain flowery phrases, are your sentences mainly crisp and staccato or languid and flowing?

Take your handwriting for instance. Does that express your personality? How would you describe it? Ask others to describe it.

Write a sentence on the three lines below.

My handwriting:

_____

_____

_____

Give a description of the personality who wrote it?

_____

_____

_____

How would others describe the personality who wrote it?

_____

_____

_____

Here's a final presentation challenge that will hone your awareness of yourself. Study yourself in the mirror for a solid five minutes. No cheating by looking away or doing it in small one minute sessions separated by an hour or so!

When you look in the mirror how would you describe what your features express?

An audience wants to see you. At the end of a Perfect Presentation it needs a sense of who you are. If you are not going to be yourself and make a difference by being there . . . send that boring old report we keep talking about!

The hardest thing is to be nobody but yourself in a world which is trying night and day to make you everybody else

e e cummings

Appearance

Just as your message is always an expression of who you are, so your physical image is naturally an extension of yourself.

Is there a satisfying relationship between: YOU, YOUR IMAGE AND YOUR MESSAGE? Your appearance for example, may need some adjustments before you can expect to be a Perfect Presenter. When you feel that you look good you probably also have an air of confidence worth far more than any designer outfit.

Audiences frequently comment on certain common

distractions:

- Buttons missing
- Hair in front of eyes
- Keys or money jangling in pockets
- Over-heavy make-up
- Pocket flaps askew
- Dated, shoddy, or creased clothes
- Stains on clothes
- Tinted spectacles
- Wisps of hair draped across bald patches

Try to be open to comments from friends about your appearance

Be willing to ask colleagues 'is there anything about the way I look that might work against my message?' Spend time in front of a mirror or video exploring the possibilities of an attractive outfit.

The apparel oft proclaims the man
William Shakespeare

Jokes and humour

As you refine your presentation you may feel it should include some touches of humour. We are sometimes asked by worried presenters for example, where does one find good jokes?

If you aren't a naturally funny person don't force yourself always to start with a joke or always use one in your presentation. Your audience will soon know if you are forcing yourself to try to be funny.

- What makes jokes funny is how they are told as much as the actual contents
- If your presentation is being simultaneously trans-

lated avoid jokes or humorous remarks which depend on language such as word play, or how the phrase is delivered
- The best jokes are situations and stories drawn from your personal experience. You have more of these available than perhaps you think
- Use your own funny bone!

I don't know jokes; I just watch the government and report the facts.
Will Rogers

PERSONALITY CHECK LIST

- Know how you come over at first impression
- Use your unique personality to make an impact
- The more you express your WHOLE self, the better presenter you will be
- Who you are, gives you permission to be the opposite
- Make sure your appearance is an expression of who you are
- Check for common distractions such as:
    Buttons missing; hair in front of eyes; keys or money jangling in pockets; over-heavy make-up; pocket flaps askew; shoddy and creased clothes; stains on clothes; tinted spectacles; wisps of hair draped across bald patches
- Ask colleagues 'is there anything about how I look that might work against my message?'
- Humour can be a good way of expressing your personality but if your presentation is being simultaneously translated, avoid jokes or humorous remarks
- The best jokes are situations and stories drawn from your personal experience

CHAPTER 4

Trouble Shooting

It happens when you least expect it. Something threatens to disrupt or even ruin your performance. Such occasions may appear unpredictable, yet you can often prepare for them. In fact, the best presenters are ready for almost anything.

What kind of problems are we talking about? Think of all the things that could go wrong with your presentation. Try listing your top 10 nightmares right now:

1 ....
2 ....
3 ....
4 ....
5 ....
6 ....
7 ....
8 ....
9 ....
10..

- How likely is this to occur and how serious would it be?

- Could its impact be reduced or even eliminated through more detailed preparation?

The mere act of going through your list of nightmare situations tends to increase your confidence as you systematically work through the implications and mentally prepare for the worst.

If something is highly unlikely to occur, it may seem obvious that you should not spend too much time preparing for that contingency. But if it did occur and would be a serious blow to your presentation, then it may well be worth thinking through how to minimise its impact.

For example, suppose you are expected to give a business presentation in a client's own building. You may not be able to do much about the effects of a fire that forces immediate evacuation. But you could certainly check whether there might be a test drill when you are scheduled to present. What would you do if it did occur?

Turning a difficult situation into a triumph is always rewarding and a sign of confidence. Increase yours in dealing with the unexpected by:

- Meticulous preparation
- Intelligent anticipation
- Readiness to improvise

Improvising means a willingness to respond positively and creatively, rather than negatively and defensively to unexpected problems. This stems partly from practice and experience but also from a willingness to take risks and think on your feet.

For example, suppose one of your nightmare scenarios is that you might go blank, completely forgetting what you are saying or what comes next. Or you may fantasise that the slide projector will die right in the middle of the presentation. Knowing roughly what you might do in such situations and even practising your response can give you enormous confidence even if the situation never arises.

Here are the basics of dealing with the unexpected:

- Don't panic! Often your audience may not even know that something has gone wrong. Take time to breathe and consider what to do next
- Focus on purpose: the more you concentrate on the overall reason for your presentation, the less likely that you will be thrown by the unexpected
- Trust yourself. You are perfectly capable of being spontaneous – it's what makes us human. Allow your natural creativity to take wing
- Use humour – this can often be a lifesaver for all kinds of presentation disasters
- Stay present. Be aware of what is happening around you so that you can respond naturally to what is needed
- Tell the truth. If something awful happens do not try and pretend it has not. Acknowledge what is happening
- Ask the audience. Involve the audience in tackling the issue and you may turn an adverse situation into one that enhances your presentation
- Risk. All presentations are a risk. If you have been thrown by a situation learn from it and move on

THE Q&A MINEFIELD

Do you dread the question and answer session? This is when a perfectly competent presentation can rapidly descend into a shambles. Basic causes include:

- Poor chairmanship
- Lack of preparation
- A tricky audience
- Time constraints
- Lack of knowledge
- Defensiveness
- Lack of respect

Useful techniques for dealing with questions include:

- Ask a colleague to give you practice by posing hard to handle questions
- Before answering, summarise the question and check that the person agrees you have understood it. This buys time and shows respect for the other person. However, use this approach sparingly, not every time you deal with a question
- Pause before responding, be seen to give it some thought – even if you know the answer instantly
- Ask the person or the audience what they think
- Invite the person to say why they have asked that particular question. If you do not know the answer be honest and say so – perhaps offer to find out and reply later
- Don't attempt to answer a whole series of questions all lumped together. Instead chose one that you can deal with well
- When you cannot match a questioner's technical mastery, acknowledge it and on behalf of the audience, invite them to put it more simply so that everyone, including you, can really understand it

CHAPTER 5

Team Presentations

The five Ps apply just as much to a team presentation. When a group has to perform together there is probably a lot at stake. So it pays to rehearse properly, rather than snatch a quick get-together on the day, or worse, do it in the taxi on your way to the venue.

Important steps in creating a powerful team presentation are:

- Choose who will lead the presentation and ensure this person practices with the entire team present
- Decide where you want the audience to focus its attention
- Clarify how the team will support this focus
- Resolve how team members will support each other
- Rehearse how each person will hand over to the next
- Identify what each person will be doing while another is speaking. Agree on how particular problems or issues will be dealt with and by whom

Roles
An effective group integrates everyone's effort into a seamless performance. Each person knows his or her

role and is confident about playing it. There are usually plenty of roles available:

- Handle questions
- Manage the visuals
- Take notes
- Watch the audience for clues
- Signal the current speaker to speak louder, softer and so on
- Chair the process by being an anchor-person

The Intro

Decide how the team will introduce itself; make sure the approach fits together. For example, if people introduce themselves separately check what they intend to say to avoid duplication and consistency of style.

A team is greater than the sum of its parts and much the same should apply to its opening introduction. Find a way to make this an interesting audience experience, rather than a boring ritual of names and titles.

For example, could you liven up the intro by making it creative and amusing? One team we know gave all the normal information about their names and titles then added what they most liked and disliked about each other!

Team Tactics

Get the team's core message clear in each person's mind. Reduce it to a single headline statement, posting it up where everyone can see it during rehearsals. This will often help eliminate confusion and uncertainty during the actual event.

Ask people to understudy each other's roles so they are comfortable about stepping in should illness or absence occur unexpectedly.

It is important that during the actual presentation everyone pays full attention to whoever is speaking. For example, there should be no fiddling with diaries or laptops, or other distractions that could divert the audience's attention.

One of the best uses of the team's time during rehearsals is to agree between you who will handle various potential disasters. What happens for example, if you are asked to do the presentation in half the allotted time? Or how will the team respond to an "expert" who challenges the group in various ways?

If possible send a presentation scout to check out the presentation environment:

- Is the venue entirely suitable?
- Any technical problems, such as inaccessible power sockets, no projector on site, an excessively large boardroom table?
- Can the lighting be adjusted?
- Where are the windows placed, might the sun shine in people's eyes?
- When will refreshments be served, at just the wrong moment?
- Can you re-arrange the tables if necessary?
- What will those attending know about the team and its company?
- How many people will attend – their names and titles?

The best team presentations are usually those where everyone participating seems to be enjoying themselves and seems willing to step out and take a risk.

CHAPTER 6

Now What?

It's over! You have done your presentation, answered all their questions and the final one for yourself is

- Did I do myself justice?

Although you will almost certainly already know the answer, it is usually worth seeking a reality check. Now is the time for some feedback.

Few of us relish criticism yet good presenters are always hungry for ways to improve and ruthlessly review their performance. A powerful way is to ask your audience directly:

- 'Did you get what you wanted?'

Or you could quietly invite comments later from selected individuals. Only by subjecting yourself to this challenging process will you learn how to perform even better next time.

Some of the post-presentation questions you can explore are:

- What went well or badly?
- What had most impact?

- What was memorable?
- Was anything confusing or unclear?
- When did I gain or lose people's attention?
- Did I do anything that annoyed or distracted?
- How would you describe my manner and tone?
- Did I seem well prepared?
- Could you hear everything I said?
- Did all the visuals work well? Which did not?
- Did I seem to care about what I said?
- Was the length too long or short?
- Did I come across with authority?

In search of the answers you might usefully view a video of your performance, or at least listen to an audio recording. Consider also inviting a professional presentation coach to assess how you come across and suggest ways to enhance your impact.

If you want to really increase your impact and your confidence it may well be worth attending a course on presenting.

Having read this book, we hope you'll begin putting your discoveries into practice. The only way to improve is through trial and error. Which brings us to a final vital point: this book is called *Perfect Presentations*. However, striving for perfection often kills spontaneity and freedom. Wanting to be perfect can be a very deadening purpose – preventing anything exciting happening. You end up focusing attention on your own judgements, rather than on your material and your audience. So, for once, we would encourage you to forget about perfection and – take risks!

Life is either a daring adventure or it's nothing.
Helen Keller

By visiting
  http://www.maynardleigh.co.uk/presenting.shtml
you can:

- Receive immediate advice, suggestions, information and stimulus about any aspect of business presentations from **The Oracle**
- Obtain useful and regularly changing presentation tips
- Extend your learning about the 5 Ps of presentation with an interactive, multi-media CD-Rom. You need a sound card for your computer and the CD offers exercises, tests, tips, web links, and other support

Additional reading
Other books you might like to dip into:

The Complete Idiot's Guide to Successful Business Presentations
Kroeger, Lin, Alpha Books, ISBN 0-02-861748-7

What to say When . . . You're dying on the Platform
Walters, Lilly, McGraw Hill, ISBN 0-07-068039-6

The Ultimate Business Presentation Book
Andrew Leigh, Random House, ISBN 0-7126-8405-0

PRESENTATION CHECK LIST

Presentation Plan
Date of assignment ....
Date of presentation ....
Number of days to prepare ....
Time of presentation...
Topic ....
Expected numbers present ....
Who is the audience ....
Remember: The communication starts with me!

The 5Ps of Powerful Presentations

Preparation

The Overall Purpose of the presentation is: ....

Have you checked content using the Full Stop
    principle?   Yes ☐ No ☐

Have you checked the technical details?   Yes ☐ No ☐

Have you checked the layout of the room, visual
    aids, etc?   Yes ☐ No ☐

Have you practised the presentation out loud?   Yes ☐ No ☐

Are you prepared for questions?   Yes ☐ No ☐

Have you thought about your appearance?   Yes ☐ No ☐

Have you prepared your voice and body warm-up? Yes ☐ No ☐

Do you have somebody to support you?   Yes ☐ No ☐

Purpose

What's the overall effect you want to have? ....

What's the moment-by-moment effect you want to have? ....

Remember: It's about building a relationship

Presence

Will you be able to check out the venue
    beforehand?   Yes ☐ No ☐

Will you be able to be 'present' there beforehand?   Yes ☐ No ☐

Remember: Highway code – stop, breathe, look, listen and feel
           Be aware
           Keep your attention on them
           Leave space

Passion

Why do *you* care about what you're saying? ....

Why should *they* care about what you're saying? ....

Personality

Remember: Be yourself (there's nobody else you can be!)
           As such, you're the perfect person to be giving this
           presentation

Performing with Presence Impact Log

Impact Ratings: 1 to 6

Event	Date	Overall	Preparation	Presence	Purpose	Passion	Personality	Notes on what went well Lessons for the future

1 = Excellent, 2 = Good, 3 = Fair, 4 = Mediocre, 5 = Poor, 6 = Disastrous